Original title:
Roots of Reflection

Copyright © 2025 Creative Arts Management OÜ
All rights reserved.

Author: Adeline Fairfax
ISBN HARDBACK: 978-1-80567-210-4
ISBN PAPERBACK: 978-1-80567-509-9

Unseen Patterns in the Wind

In a garden of socks, where the bluebirds dwell,
A dance is unfolding, oh who can tell?
The daisies are gossiping, petals all aflutter,
While the wind tickles noses, causing a stutter.

Marigolds chuckle, so bold and bright,
As the clouds swirl above, what a comical sight!
A butterfly sneezes, while bees make a fuss,
Spinning tales in the air, full of humor and truss.

The sun shares a wink with a tree on the hill,
As shadows stretch long, the laughter won't chill.
A breeze sings a tune that's slightly off-key,
But hey, it's the effort, it's quite free!

So here in this chaos, where nonsense is king,
We find silly patterns, oh what joy they bring!
In a world of surprises, where laughter takes flight,
The unseen connects us, from day into night.

The Depths of Still Waters

In still waters, thoughts do sway,
A fish with glasses swam today.
He pondered life as bubbles rise,
And how to wear a clever disguise.

A turtle told him, slow is right,
But tripped on seaweed in fright.
They laughed at waves that couldn't glide,
While seahorses danced side by side.

A Journey to the Core

An apple fell with quite a thud,
Claiming wisdom in the mud.
Its core said, "I'm quite profound!"
Yet seeds just giggled underground.

For every bite the world can take,
There's juice of joy that we can make.
With each dig in, discovery found,
Yet still, that worm spun round and round.

Threads of Existence

A spider spun a web with flair,
In hopes a fly would find a chair.
But all that came were ants in line,
Forming conga lines, oh so fine!

The sticky threads, a party trap,
Where mischief danced and laughter tapped.
But spiders need their peace and space,
Not ants in togas at the base.

Footprints in Silence

In winter's hush, a track appears,
Left by a penguin who feared cheers.
He waddled fast, then took a pause,
And slipped right by with quite a cause!

His buddies laughed till snowflakes fell,
As he embarked on silent yell.
But each soft print in fresh white snow,
Told tales of trips that stole the show.

The Soil Speaks in Silence

The dirt once whispered tales so bold,
Of worms in suits, and ants made of gold.
They chuckled at seeds, so naive and shy,
While tipsy roots danced, asking why?

A potato claimed it once stole the show,
While cabbage swayed, putting on a toe.
In earthy revelry, they laughed and rolled,
The soil held secrets, as the stories told.

Elixirs of the Past

In a bottle of jam, the past resides,
With strawberries arguing, and raspberries slides.
A pickle jar filled with dad's weird schemes,
While olives debate the craziest dreams.

Tomatoes in sauce, jesters on a spree,
Whispering 'bout laughter, as sweet as can be.
The elixirs of bygone giggles and spills,
Every taste a memory, giving us chills.

Beneath the Moonlit Canopy

Beneath the stars, the owls have a ball,
Telling old jokes that still make us fall.
A squirrel in a tux, attending a dance,
While shouting, 'I swear, it's just circumstantial chance!'

The shadows do waltz, with light as a tease,
While branches gossip about whispers in trees.
A raccoon breaks in, to steal all the snacks,
'This party's wild!' he gleefully cracks.

Shadows of Yesteryears

In the attic, a ghost tries to tell a joke,
But nobody laughs, he's a dreadful bloke.
He fumbles with dust, plays hide and seek,
While old hats giggle, feeling very chic.

Forgotten toys reminisce about their fame,
As marbles and soldiers play the blame game.
Shadows gather around, all friends in delight,
Recalling their heyday, a comical sight.

The Pulse of Hidden Histories

In the attic, boxes stacked high,
Old shoes that squeak, they say goodbye.
Grandma's yarn, tangled and bold,
Whispers of secrets, too shy to be told.

A hat that fits a clown's wide grin,
Memories dance like they're made of tin.
Photographs fade, but who's to blame?
We laugh at the faces—wait, who's that same?

Dust bunnies shyly peek from the cracks,
Each one holds stories, they've done their hacks.
Pots and pans sing a clanging song,
Chefs in training, always getting it wrong.

So here's to the past that always comes back,
Like lost luggage on a confusing track.
We poke and we prod at our family lore,
With laughter and jest, always wanting more!

Reverberations in the Stillness

The clock ticks loudly, can't you hear?
Whispers of time stuck on repeat, dear.
Granpa's chair creaks a comedic tune,
While Aunt June's cat is plotting to swoon.

We see the echoes of antics gone wild,
Uncle Joe's wig, oh—so very mild.
Laughter hangs thick in the air like smoke,
As cousin Sam pulls his age-old joke.

The garden sprouts tales, weeds and wishes,
Bumblebees buzzing, sweet little fishes.
Nature sighs softly, a giggle behind,
When the squirrels steal snacks, oh what a find!

So join the dance on this humorous ride,
Where memories shimmer and laughter won't hide.
In stillness, you'll find a playful embrace,
As we chase the hilarity—let's pick up the pace!

A Symphony of Lost Moments

In a concert hall where socks go missing,
A symphony played—not quite a blessing.
The cat on the piano hits a flat note,
While the dog learns to dance, just to gloat.

Each missed cue brings a chuckle or two,
As the audience laughs, folks in a stew.
Clarinet players are tangled in cords,
And stage fright hits harder than blooper rewards.

The taps of the shoes create tunes so funny,
That even the moon chuckles, isn't it honey?
A trumpet blares loud with a raspberry sound,
And suddenly, laughter's the best part around.

So raise your glass to the rhythm of jest,
In the orchestra of life, we're truly blessed.
From lost moments, a melody stems,
As we dance in the chaos, life's little gems.

The Embrace of Time's Emotions

Time in a bottle—oh, what a sight,
Full of mischief, it's taken to flight.
Mom's old diary spills secrets galore,
About how she swiped dad's snacks from the store.

Tick-tock, it seems time's gone a bit mad,
Where the fridge holds mysteries that make us glad.
An old rubber chicken hangs on the wall,
Reminds us of laughter that echoes through halls.

From silly socks that don't match in style,
To stories that leave us with a big, goofy smile,
Each moment's an emotion, so vivid and bright,
Like popcorn that pops in the depths of the night.

So dance with the years like they're silly ballet,
Embrace all the joy, come what may.
For in the embrace of each tick and each tock,
We find our own rhythm—let laughter unlock!

Memories in the Underbrush

In the thicket, I found my shoe,
A squirrel mocked me, what could I do?
With tangled thoughts and a madcap dash,
I tripped on life's own leafy stash.

Laughter bubbled up like spring rain,
Each mishap danced with a silly refrain.
The past is a treasure, half-buried and dense,
Digging it up feels like pure suspense.

Toadstools sprouted wisdom, or so I would say,
Who knew my grass stains had lessons to relay?
Chasing shadows in a wild goose chase,
My memories frolic in a cheeky embrace.

So here's to the moments that made me a clown,
With roots of mischief, I'll never back down!
In a forest of laughter, I'll surely explore,
Finding comedic gems, oh, there's always more!

In the Heart of Memory

In the heart where giggles grow,
I found old cheese, don't ask me how, though.
A whimsical relic from long, long ago,
I pondered its age, while my pet cat meowed.

Here lies a photo, us with big grins,
Twirled in a blender of blunders and spins.
Oh, the dance moves! A sight to be seen,
More like a giraffe than a graceful machine.

With each snapshot, a treasure unfolds,
Golden memories wrapped in pure silliness bold.
Jellybeans in pockets, a mischief spree,
Lost in the laughter; come join in, you'll see!

So here's to the memories that tickle the soul,
In this crazy carnival, let's lose control.
For in laughter we find, oh so crafty and true,
The sweet joy of living, just waiting for you!

Threads of Yesterday

Woven in laughter, with joys left behind,
Drift about like a kite, totally unconfined.
I stitched together snippets, bright as can be,
Like spaghetti that danced just to annoy me!

Each tidbit recalls a quirk that we knew,
Like Grandma's hat, or that pie made of glue.
The patterns we fashion from threads of our play,
Make a patchwork of giggles that brighten the day.

Remember that time we swapped shoes in the park?
Did we really believe we could kickstart a lark?
With mismatched sandals and laughs in the air,
Who knew footwear could spark so much flair?

So here's to the threads, both tangled and neat,
In the quilt of our lives, they're the craziest treat.
With every stitch, let's make sure we know,
That laughter is timeless, a zany tableau!

A Mosaic of Fleeting Light

In a sunbeam of chaos, I found my old hat,
Adorned with bright feathers, a real chatty brat.
It laughed and it danced, with a twirl and a spin,
Who knew my headgear held secrets within?

That late-night snack turned gourmet delight,
Is that pizza lurking, or just a lost bite?
With unicorn dreams on a plate made of gold,
Memories glimmer, more precious than mold.

The flicker of laughter, a mosaic so clear,
Each piece of my past brings both joy and some fear.
Bouncing through time like a wild fleeting sprite,
I find giggles bloom in the strangest of sights.

So here's to the magic, the light and the sound,
Each bright little moment where silliness found.
In this playful adventure, both silly and bright,
Let's cherish the chaos, our mosaic of light!

The Rapture of Forgotten Tales

Once upon a time, as stories go,
A chicken crossed paths with a wily crow.
They squabbled over breadcrumbs, oh what a fight,
While squirrels took bets on the fowl's last night.

In the blink of an eye, the sun took a dive,
A wise old turtle said, 'Let's just survive!'
The rooster laid down his feathered pride,
As they shared a laugh and the crumbs worldwide.

Laughter echoed through the rustling grass,
The woes of the day slipped on by like glass.
Fables stitched together with wild, wacky things,
So here's to the tales that giggle and sing!

Then came a cat, with her sly, twitchy nose,
She purred, "A party's in store, who knows?"
So the jests cascaded like leaves on a breeze,
In the rapture of tales, our hearts found ease.

In the Heart of Stillness

In a quiet corner, a snail wore a hat,
He pondered the meaning of a well-done spat.
Meanwhile, a wise owl was counting to ten,
For the yoga class with the frogs and the hen.

The stillness brought giggles, a breeze filled the air,
As grasshoppers danced without a single care.
The moon winked down, with a grin on its face,
Watching the chaos of this slow-paced race.

A turtle declared with a smile so wide,
"Life's just a ride if you take it in stride!"
But the rabbit hopped in, with a dash and a spin,
Claiming all motion was a win, win, win!

So amidst all the calm, a ruckus arose,
With laughter and antics from toes to the nose.
In the heart of stillness, joy had no end,
And a world made of fun held each creature as friend.

The Hidden Ways

In a thicket of whispers, the hedgehogs conspire,
To start a small circus, with acts to inspire.
They juggled with apples, with gusto and flair,
While a dapper old crow tossed confetti in the air.

Each critter had secrets, of spectacles grand,
The tortoise balanced a fish on his hand.
With a backflip so fancy, the rabbits all cheered,
For the show of the century, all laughter appeared.

But the flowers were jealous, their petals in rage,
They plotted a heist on the grand little stage.
With petals like hijackers, they danced through the night,
Stealing the spotlight, oh what a delight!

In the hidden ways, where the silly things grew,
Each creature and flower danced under the blue.
For laughter is treasure, it bubbles and sways,
In a world made of whimsy, we'll find hidden ways.

Fragments of the Ancient Heart

In the shadows of history, a frog wrote a tome,
Of ancient adventures; he felt far from home.
He croaked of the times when the world was a stage,
When the gossiping owls scribbled words on a page.

With fragments of laughter, the tales danced around,
Of knights in the leafy woods, lost and found.
A dragon in slippers, a lizard with style,
Made all the historians chuckle and smile.

The jesters bounced in with their jingling caps,
While dancing on tabletops, sharing mishaps.
For the tale of the heart is a riddle divine,
Made for all creatures, from rabbit to swine.

And in fragments of moments, the laughter we share,
Connects all the stories we've hidden with care.
So let's toast to the folly that life oft imparts,
For joy is the essence of these ancient hearts.

Anchored in the Silence

In a garden of whispers, I stand so still,
The gnomes wave at me, it's quite a thrill.
My thoughts float like bubbles, they pop and they sway,
As I ponder the snacks I forgot on the tray.

The flowers giggle softly, dressed in their best,
They've seen all my blunders, they know all the jest.
A bee lands to gossip, just buzzing away,
And I laugh with the daisies, come join in the fray.

The Depths of Recollection

In the depths of my mind, old memories loom,
Like socks missing partners, they're lost in the gloom.
I dig with a shovel, what treasures I'll find,
A picture of me, in green pants, unconfined.

I rummage through moments, they dance and they spin,
A cat wearing glasses, where's my brain been?
I chuckle at missteps and giggles galore,
As I ponder the potluck and my dish turned to pour.

A Journey Through the Soil

Sifting through secrets, I follow the trail,
Past worms in their tuxedos, ready to sail.
The moles hold a gala beneath the hard ground,
I'm invited for tea, with snacks all around.

Digging deeper for giggles, I stumble on snails,
With stories of travel, on leaf-shaped trails.
I laugh as I wander through earth's playful jest,
In this quirky museum, I feel truly blessed.

Reflections Beneath the Canopy

Under the tall trees, shadows break out in cheer,
The squirrels stage musicals, offering a beer.
Their acorn hats tilted, they dance and they prance,
While I sit on a log, joining in on their dance.

The canopy whispers, like gossiping friends,
In this leafy lounge where the laughter never ends.
A breeze carries chuckles, I sip from my mug,
And realize my thoughts aren't as tight as a rug.

Chronicles of the Soul

In the attic of my mind,
Old socks and dreams intertwine.
A duck with a monocle sits,
Quacking jokes that give me fits.

Peering into some dusty chests,
Finding shirts that were my best,
They whisper secrets, laugh a bit,
Telling tales where I've misplaced it.

A pizza slice with a crown,
Sits on my head, why so down?
It claims that it's a royal feast,
But it's just grease, not a beast.

So here I am, laughing bright,
Chasing shadows, oh, what a sight.
Life's a circus, full of clowns,
And I'm just here wearing frowns.

In the Quiet Grove

Under trees with twisted lore,
Squirrels debate, what's life for?
A leaf falls down, dressed in plaid,
It's the best fashion choice I've had.

A chipmunk juggles acorns wide,
Telling tales with great pride.
While grass whispers secrets fair,
And insects dance without a care.

A gopher tiptoes, looking sly,
In a top hat, oh my oh my!
It steals my sandwich with a grin,
Quickly darts away, such a sin!

In this grove where laughter grows,
I find joy in friends and foes.
With every giggle, every quirk,
Nature's humor does its work.

Gazing into the Mosaic

Pieces of a life unmade,
Stickers stuck, colors delayed.
A toaster dreams of being deep,
While pancakes plot their secret leap.

Fragments here, and bits of there,
A rubber chicken with a glare.
It honks, it dances, what a scene,
In this jigsaw fit for a queen.

Every shard with stories loud,
Even dust has a quirky crowd.
My coffee mug, an artist proud,
Paints splashes that make laughter shroud.

In this puzzle, I collide,
With silly thoughts I cannot hide.
Each piece a giggle, each part, a dance,
In the chaos, I find my chance.

Fragmented Mirrors

Reflecting back a goofy grin,
My hair's a lion, let the day begin.
This mirror laughs, it bends and shakes,
Hiding secrets of my mistakes.

A warped view of socks unmatched,
One striped, one polka, both dispatched.
As I stand in front of the glass,
It giggles loudly, as I sass.

My smile won't fit in this frame,
It stretches wide, oh what a game!
Each crack holds some quirky lore,
Echoes of fun, who could ask for more?

With each glance, I find new wonder,
Dancing shadows make me ponder.
In these shards, my true self gleams,
Woven in laughter, stitched with dreams.

Echoing Through the Ages

In the attic, dusty boxes lie,
Memories whisper, oh so sly.
Old socks once worn, now a treasure,
Of lost time, they bring great pleasure.

Granddad's tales of skinned knees,
And grandma's dance that brought him to tease.
Half-finished puzzles stacked high,
Who knew they were made for a pie in the sky?

A mirror cracked, reflects the jest,
Of family quirks—truly the best.
Every laugh echoes, bouncing about,
In this space where we dance and shout.

The Understory of Identity

Beneath the surface, the giggles thrive,
Where old jokes bubble, keeping us alive.
There's Uncle Joe, with his hat so wide,
Said he'd win the race but tripped on pride.

Our family tree's a winding tale,
Of mischief and memories that never pale.
A cousin's face with whipped cream surprise,
How nostalgia comes wrapped in wide-eyed lies.

With every photo, stories unfurl,
The denim dance of a twirling girl.
From unkempt locks to laughter bright,
The humor in us is a pure delight.

Silent Conversations with the Past

In a room with shadows that seem to sneak,
Whispers float by, we can't help but peek.
A grandpa's pipe still curls in the air,
While grandma's apron sways with her flair.

In ghostly whispers, tales do unfold,
About sock monsters and secrets bold.
Alas, silent tales with a splash of glee,
Can't forget that time they lost the key!

With every corner, a chuckle left behind,
The echoes of moments—so lovingly kind.
A wink from the past, we tiptoe in tune,
These laughable ghosts are our joy in this room.

Music from the Hidden Roots

Beneath the floorboards, a racket they make,
The tunes of the past, wide-awake.
With pots for drums and old forks as spoons,
They dance through the night under vibrant moons.

Rhythms of laughter, cheers that invade,
Kitchen concert filled with love and tirade.
Who knew the blender could croon so sweet?
Even the toaster joins with a pop and a beat!

From echoes of chuckles to rhythmic vibrations,
Hidden melodies spark generations.
In their laughter, we find our refrain,
Music flows deep like the family's vein.

Unraveling the Forgotten

In the attic of my mind, I found,
A rubber chicken wearing a crown.
Dust bunnies twirled in a merry dance,
While old socks giggled in a silly trance.

Memories tangled like old earphones,
Whispering secrets in hushed tones.
My childhood toys laughed at the sight,
Of my grown-up self losing the fight.

Forgotten dreams peeked from behind,
With a wink and a nudge, oh so unkind.
They tossed confetti, and off they flew,
Chasing the past, if only I knew.

So here's to the mess that we all keep,
A treasure trove when we dare to peek.
In the chaos, humor takes the lead,
As laughter sprouts from the strangest seed.

In the Soil of the Soul

Deep in the garden of my heart,
Worms debate on who's the best part.
Daisies gossip, and daisies tease,
While the weeds plot mischief with such ease.

Sunflowers dance with a dapper flair,
Brushing each other with crisp spring air.
But underneath, in the muck and mire,
Lie snickers and giggles, ripe with desire.

The carrots claim they're the star of the show,
While turnips prance with an exaggerated glow.
In the soil, secrets are buried deep,
Where laughter and dreams often leap.

So let's plant joy to harvest the fun,
In this quirky patch, we've barely begun.
Let's laugh at what sprouts, whatever it may,
In the soil of the soul, we'll fashion our play.

Remnants of What Once Was

In the cupboard of yesterday, things went awry,
Old takeout boxes whisper, "Oh, my!"
A carton of milk wearing a tuxedo grin,
Says, "It's not my fault that things used to be thin!"

Mismatched spoons, singing a loud tune,
Dreaming of parties beneath the full moon.
Napkins remember the spills and the stains,
While forks recount tales of glorious gains.

The cereal boxes hold wild debates,
Arguing flavors like old dinner mates.
Soggy memories linger on every shelf,
As I chuckle and grin at my foolish self.

So, lift a toast to the old and bizarre,
To the mishaps and laughter—how strange we are.
In remnants of what was, giggles we'll find,
A treasure of humor, where we're all intertwined.

The Heart's Hidden Path

Somewhere in laughter, there lies a road,
Paved with giggles and stories untold.
Where hiccups turn into comedy nights,
And failures become our most cherished rites.

The path twists and turns, but who really cares?
For clowns chase the raindrops, shedding their wares.
With each silly step on this crazy track,
I find joy and humor, never looking back.

With a hop and a skip, I'm a fool for the fun,
Dancing with shadows 'til the day is done.
The heart knows its rhythm, no fear in the fray,
As laughter guides me, come what may.

So let's wander together in jests and in glee,
On the heart's hidden path, just you and me.
Embrace every chuckle, each joyous reprieve,
Finding the magic in all that we believe.

Echoes from the Wellspring

In the depths where giggles grow,
Bubbles burst with tales to show.
Silly fish swim round and round,
Giggling softly, joy unbound.

Water dances, splashes bright,
Making waves by sheer delight.
Reflections leap, they twist and shout,
Here's the fun, there's no doubt!

Mirthful murmurs through the stream,
Tickling dreams that make us beam.
A splash of laughter, oh so sweet,
Where every ripple brings a treat.

The wellspring smiles, it knows the game,
With every quirk, no thought of fame.
So dive right in, don't fear the splash,
This pool of joy is quite a bash!

Beneath the Bark

Underneath the clever trees,
Squirrels plot with sneaky ease.
Barking orders, nuts in tow,
Wit as sharp as winter's snow.

Leaves are giggling in the breeze,
Telling tales of playful tease.
Bark that whispers, oh so sly,
"Here comes trouble, quick, oh my!"

Roots are dancing, what a sight,
Tapping rhythms day and night.
Nature's jesters in their play,
Make the solemn fade away.

So when you stroll through woods so grand,
Hear the laughter all around.
Join the fun, let spirits rise,
Life's a joke, to our surprise!

Fragments of a Timeless Whisper

Whispers travel on the breeze,
Carrying secrets, quirks, and tease.
A cheeky breeze with tales to say,
"Life's a joke, come laugh and play!"

Tickling sands on the shore,
Grains of giggles, laughter's score.
Each fragment tells a wobbly tale,
Of seaweed dancers and fishy trail.

Clouds chatter in puffy glee,
Making shadows, wild and free.
If you catch their tipsy dance,
You might just join their laughter's chance.

So tune your ears to whispers near,
Find the humor in each cheer.
Fragments of joy in every sigh,
Remind us that we can't just fly!

The Heart's Umbra

Underneath the glowing sun,
Shadows stretch and start to run.
With a jump and playful twist,
Even shadows can't resist.

Umbrella thoughts that twist and twirl,
A heart that flutters like a girl.
Every shade has jokes to share,
Spinning round for fun and flair.

Ticklish jokes in moonlit nights,
With every splash, a giggle ignites.
The heart knows how to dance along,
In every pulse, there's a song.

So when the dark creeps in to play,
Dance with shadows, don't delay.
For even in the deepest dark,
A funny twist will leave a mark!

The Hidden Portrait

In the attic dust bunnies bounce,
Grandma's old portraits do pounce.
With a goofy smile and a wink,
I swear she taught the cat to think.

Frames all askew, like a funhouse maze,
Each glance leads to delightful daze.
A mustache here, a wig on a head,
Was that supposed to be an old bread?

Mirrors giggle, whispering lies,
These old reflections crackup and rise.
What tales they tell, once crystal clear,
Now just echoes that make us cheer!

So much laughter in layers of dust,
In every crack, find joy we trust.
Portraits hidden, yet out in the light,
Who knew nostalgia could be such a sight?

Beneath Worn Trails

Beneath the tracks where shadows play,
Lost items meet their disarray.
Old boots laugh when no one's near,
Who knew soles could have such cheer?

A wobble in the bicycle lane,
Old tires mutter, 'We'll ride again.'
Stickers peeling, tales unfold,
Each scratch is worth its weight in gold.

Scooters squeak like chatty mice,
They share their secrets, oh so nice.
Pavement maps of childish glee,
Unearth the laughs, set the spirit free!

So let us roam on paths once traced,
In laughter's grip, we're all embraced.
Each step a tickle, tickling wit,
With worn-out trails, we all commit.

The Caress of Ancient Breezes

Whispers float on the old oak's sway,
Breezes tease in the light of day.
They rustle leaves, snicker and glide,
Telling tales of those who've tried.

A squirrel winks from up on high,
While the winds giggle, passing by.
Each gust a joke, a playful jest,
Who knew the air could be so blessed?

Dandelions dance, silly in flight,
Tickling noses, just out of sight.
'Catch me if you can!' they call with glee,
As ancient gusts set memories free.

With each soft puff, smiles arise,
Reminders of laughter beneath the skies.
Oh, to be light like those breezes pure,
Crafting chuckles, that's the allure!

A Canvas of Memories

In the basement lies an old crate,
Filled with colors of love and fate.
Bright paint splatters, giggles from ages,
Each stroke a story, turning pages.

Mismatched brushes, one lost his way,
But adds to the chaos we love to play.
With every smear, a tale appears,
Who knew art was mixed with our tears?

Canvas whispers of splendor and fun,
Portraits of mischief under the sun.
Footprints in paint, a rainbow of strife,
Each crooked line sings of life.

So let's splash and daub till the end,
With each blot, our hearts we'll mend.
In the gallery of giggles and cheer,
The canvas of memories, forever dear.

Beneath the Surface

In the pond, a frog does leap,
He thinks he's grand, a prince so deep.
With lily pads as his fine throne,
He croaks out jokes, all on his own.

A fish swims by and gives a wink,
'That froggy humor—what do you think?'
The bubbles rise, they float and dance,
While water bugs roll their eyes at chance.

As shadows play beneath the waves,
The antics of this pond, it saves.
Reflections giggle, ripple wide,
In this silly splash, all take pride.

So when you're down, just take a dive,
Join the pond, where laughs arrive!
For life is bright, and all's a jest,
In wet domain, we are quite blessed.

A Tapestry of Time

Grandpa's tales are quite a stitch,
They twist and turn, sometimes a glitch.
He starts at noon, ends with a yawn,
In every tale, a gag is drawn.

With every thread, a twisty fate,
A cat who danced with a plate of cake.
The fabric glows with laughter loud,
As every family joke is proud.

A goldfish named Bob runs for mayor,
Promising treats and an endless prayer.
Yet when elections bring a fuss,
Bob curls back, not making a fuss.

So gather 'round, weave stories tight,
Each silly moment brings such delight.
Life's a riot, stitched with care,
In humor's weave, we all can share.

Where the Old Dreams Dwell

In an attic, dusty dreams reside,
A cow jumped high, oh what a ride!
With hats that spin and shoes that dance,
These memories giggle, given a chance.

A picture frame, with faces so bright,
That wink back at you in the night.
They whisper tales of wild imaginations,
Where socks host balls and cats lead nations.

A rocking chair creaks with a grin,
Telling secrets of where it's been.
With every rock, the stories unfold,
Of laughter shared and memories bold.

So venture up to dusty old skies,
And breathe in laughter that never dies.
In corners cozy, where dreams still hover,
Find the giggles—and welcome each other!

Images in the Water

The puddles laugh when the skies pour,
Showing reflections of tales galore.
With ducks that quack and jump around,
Each splash creates new laughter found.

A kid runs by, boots on tight,
Leaps into the puddle—oh, what a sight!
With droplets flying, a rainbow made,
A giggly symphony, nature's parade.

Images dance, like silly gnomes,
As water paints whimsical homes.
A swan preens with a snickered grace,
In this liquid realm, they find their place.

So next time storms bring forth a flood,
Embrace the joy, go splashing in mud!
For in the chaos, laughter flows,
In puddles deep, the joy just grows.

Underneath the Growing Canopy

In the shade where shadows play,
Squirrels dance in a silly way,
Leaves whisper secrets, oh so bright,
While birds crack jokes from morning's light.

Beneath the branches, laughter sings,
A chorus made of feathered things,
Nutty tales from acorn heads,
Dreams of naps in soft, green beds.

Twisting roots like tangled socks,
Growing dreams just like old clocks,
Mushrooms giggle, fungi cheer,
Underneath, there's nothing to fear.

So come, recline beneath the shade,
In this garden, joy's parade,
With silly bugs and flowers too,
Life's a laugh, just like a zoo.

Traces of Time's Embrace

Tickle the trunks, they might just laugh,
Old man oak is quite the chaff,
Bark so wrinkled tells of years,
While critters poke and tease their peers.

Each ring a giggle, each knot a joke,
Time's a clown, just look, it pokes,
Whispers echo under the sky,
As wind-flecked giggles flutter by.

As branches sway, the crows all caw,
They're reeling in tales of nature's law,
Time tiptoes, playing hide and seek,
While shadows of laughter play and peek.

A racing breeze, a playful tease,
Floating seeds like confetti, if you please,
With echoes of time that can't be caught,
We wander off, leaving thoughts in rot.

Inward Mirrors

Looking deep in a puddle's grin,
Who's that silly face within?
A bounce of light caught in a splash,
Reflections dance in a jolly flash.

Thoughts ripple like a pebble tossed,
Making waves at laughter's cost,
Each splash a giggle, each wave a joke,
Who knew water could be such folk?

Mirror, mirror, on the ground,
Where laughter's echo is found,
A wavering thought, a fishy wink,
Revealing more than we might think.

With splashes bright and giggles near,
Jump right in, release your fear,
In every dip, a new surprise,
As inward mirrors wink and rise.

Seeds of Memory

Dancing seeds on the breeze do twirl,
Like tiny fairies in a whirl,
Each little puff tells a tale,
Of joyful trips and silly trails.

They tumble down, making jokes anew,
Whispering giggles, just me and you,
In grassy patches, they poked their heads,
Inventing fun in all the spreads.

With a sprinkle and flutter, their stories unfold,
Of sunshine glasses and moments bold,
Bouncing through gardens, laughter's cheer,
Memories sprout with good friends near.

So plant a whim, let it grow wild,
In this funny game, we're all a child,
With seeds of joy and hugs of glee,
Let's cherish our laughter, you and me.

Whispers of the Ancestors

In the attic, dust bunnies play,
Grandpa's jokes still find their way.
Old chairs creak in laughter's tune,
Echoing tales beneath the moon.

A family tree with quirky limbs,
Uncle Joe danced on a whim.
Auntie's hat, a sight to behold,
When she swore she'd never be old!

Photos hang on the wall so bright,
With mustaches that just seem polite.
Cousins giggle, secrets to share,
As we reminisce without a care.

The echoes tease, the memories dance,
Laughter plays in every glance.
Who knew history could be such fun?
Join the laughter; let's all run!

Echoes Beneath the Surface

In the garden, gnomes take a peek,
Whispered secrets to those who seek.
Worms wiggle in the soil so nice,
It's a party, no need for advice!

Tales of roots beneath our feet,
Where the weird and wacky often meet.
A squirrel steals acorns with grace,
While the raccoons just make a face.

Old wooden benches hold their ground,
With stories of laughter all around.
Nellie's plants grow in wild array,
She swears they dance when she goes away!

The echoes laugh, they twist and shout,
As bugs and blooms all round about.
Digging deep into the dirt,
Life's a joke, and oh, how we flirt!

The Tapestry Within

In every thread, a color bright,
Patterns twist in morning light.
Grandma stitched a funny face,
Said it brings good luck and grace.

Each stitch tells of tales so bold,
From sock puppets to stories told.
Uncle Bob's pants might be too tight,
But at least he dances with all his might!

Laughter weaves through every seam,
Like a crazy, patchwork dream.
Each fiber whispers a funny note,
As siblings share a silly quote.

Oh, the knots that twist and turn,
In every laugh, there's much to learn.
Life's full of fun, stitch it well,
With each funny tale we tell!

Shadows of My History

In the shadow of my comfy chair,
Lives a past that's full of flair.
Distant relatives with wild style,
Make me laugh and stay awhile.

Their antics, oh, what pure delight,
Twirling ghosts in the soft moonlight.
A great-aunt's wig that flew away,
Left everyone in fits that day!

Pictures curl at the edges now,
With happy faces that all say 'wow.'
A sibling slipped and fell in goo,
And Aunt Edna laughed right on cue!

These shadows dance, they jig and prance,
In histories that weave a chance.
To find the joy in every flip,
And in the laughter, take a trip!

Resilient Tendrils

In the garden, sprouting hope,
Wiggly dreams, a slippery slope.
Beneath the soil, they dig and play,
Turning troubles into clay.

With laughter spreading, skies so blue,
They dance with worms, just a crew.
Twists and turns in merry delight,
Claiming shadows as their right.

In the Hushed Thicket

In the thicket, whispers thrive,
Squirrels chuckle, barely alive.
Branches bend, a bit of sass,
Nature's jokes, a playful class.

Here the bunnies claim their ground,
Jumping high, not making sound.
A secret world, where giggles hide,
Under leaves, where dreams collide.

Portraits Embraced by Time

Painted faces in the dust,
Old tales linger, they must trust.
Time's tickle on every line,
Chasing moments, sweet and fine.

In the echoes, laughter rings,
Whimsical hearts and fleeting flings.
Each wrinkle tells a funny grace,
Memories dance like a painted face.

Germination of Forgotten Dreams

In the dark, where dreams do sleep,
Funny thoughts begin to creep.
Sprouting out with a goofy grin,
Who knew plans could make us spin?

Tiny seeds, they plot and scheme,
Waking up from a crazy dream.
Chasing sunlight, a comical chase,
Growing wild in a jumbled place.

The Legacy Beneath the Bark

Once a sturdy tree stood tall,
Claimed by squirrels, it had a ball.
Bark covered history, laughs untold,
As wise old owls recounted, bold.

From branches wide to roots that twist,
Mice made plans on a sunlit list.
Each not-so-silent whisper grew,
"The acorns? We'll stash them! Who knew?"

Between the ferns, tales grew grand,
Of the wind's pranks, a mischievous hand.
In this comedy of flora and fauna,
Nuts in their cheeks, a laughable drama.

So next time you stroll, don't you smile?
The trees are chuckling all the while!
For beneath every bark, so absurd,
Lies a legacy that's hardly heard.

To Dance with Shadows

In the moonlight, shadows prance,
A waltz of whispers, a cheeky dance.
The crickets join with a rhythm bold,
Squirrels mimicking, brave and uncontrolled.

Beneath the yews, a pair takes flight,
Chasing each other in the soft twilight.
"Did you see that? Who stepped on my toe?"
"Not me! Blame the owl, always in tow!"

A playful breeze makes the branches sway,
It tickles the leaves, come out to play!
As shadows laugh and giggle away,
In the quiet, mischief holds sway.

So dance with the dark, don't be shy,
With giggles and gasps that soar to the sky.
For in shadow's embrace, delight takes hold,
As nature crafts stories, both silly and bold.

Illuminated Paths of Old

Once, down the lane, lanterns would fade,
Guided by laughter, secrets conveyed.
Fireflies sparkled in a burst of cheer,
While bunnies conspired, "Not us, my dear!"

The old oak remembered those midnight glows,
And the oddities bouncing on tiny toes.
"Did you trip again? You're quite the player!"
"Only because the shadows got braver!"

On those paths, stories intertwined,
A hedgehog's cartwheel through leaves, aligned.
With giggling puddles and sly, sneaky creeks,
An adventure like magic, nature cheekily speaks.

So cherish those moments, embrace the delight,
For magic waits in the dead of night.
Old paths illuminate tales anew,
With each step you take, a chuckle will brew.

A Palimpsest in Nature

Underneath layers of green and gold,
Histories whisper, wild stories unfold.
A patch of daisies with wisecrack flair,
Glimpse the past blooms with laughter to share.

Once a tall fern made a fashion faux pas,
Called out by daisies, "You never saw?"
It fluffed up, proud, "I'm the trendiest here!"
But laughed at the wiggle of a passing deer.

Leaves exchange gossip, a fluttering chirp,
As ants pass by with a well-timed burp.
Each crack in the soil spins tales of its own,
Of critters and frolics, once overthrown.

So take a good look at what's underneath,
Nature, hilarious, always bequeaths.
In every wrinkle, every twist and bend,
Lies a palimpsest where jests never end.

Reveries of the Ancients

In a land where echoes giggle and sway,
Ancient spirits dance in the light of day.
They juggle with memories, tossing them high,
Telling tall tales of how they learned to fly.

With each twist and turn of their silly parade,
They point to the sun, where their humor is made.
A mishap with shadows, they cackle and spin,
In the laughter of ages, where the fun begins.

Traces of a Woven Heart

In a stitch-up of giggles, the fabric gets taut,
Weaves of the past tickle, oh what a thought!
Laughter and yarn, what a jolly old mix,
They craft quirky stories, all filled with tricks.

Each thread carries whispers of blunders and glee,
A patchwork of folly, come join for a spree!
As voices entwine in a tangled ballet,
They're knitting sweet chaos in the silliest way.

Threads of the Forgotten

Once upon a tapestry thick with a twist,
Forgotten yarns giggle, they simply can't resist.
Each fiber a tale of mishaps and cheer,
Threads of the past whisper jokes in your ear.

They clash with delight in a wild sort of dance,
Stitching together what fate let askance.
From silly missteps to blunders so grand,
The fabric unravels with a wave of the hand.

The Garden of Lost Thoughts

In a garden of giggles where thoughts bloom and sprout,
Lost ideas frolic, they leap in and out.
They tickle your mind, oh what a delight,
A riot of nonsense, springing up day and night.

With weeds made of laughter, they twist and they turn,
Every corner a chuckle, bright lessons to learn.
Amidst the rubber trees with wisdom absurd,
The joy of the silly is never unheard.

The Tides of Time

Waves crash with a giggle, don't you see?
They tickle our toes, like wild, silly glee.
The clock spins in circles, wearing a hat,
Time's a jester, imagine that!

Moments slide by in a slippery dance,
We chase after laughter, taking a chance.
Each second's a prank, a joke to unfold,
A treasure of cheer that never gets old.

Past memories tease like a playful breeze,
Tickling our minds with such strange expertise.
We laugh at the wrinkles that age can bestow,
But really, we know, it's just time's funny show.

So let's ride this tide, in joy we will flow,
With laughter as our guide, we'll steal the show.
For each tick of the clock brings a grin, it seems,
Life's just a series of whimsical dreams.

A Requiem for Forgotten Footsteps

Once I trod paths, with shoes untied,
Where are those footprints? Ah, they've all sighed.
The soles of my shoes keep playing hide and seek,
They laugh while I ponder the days that seem bleak.

Each step was a mishap, a trip and a fall,
I gathered the stories of stumbling small.
Forgotten escapades now shine out of reach,
Like socks with no partners, or lessons to teach.

The echoes of laughter linger quite strong,
While memories chirp like a silly old song.
But life takes the lead, and the dance never ends,
With jigs and with jests, as our humor transcends.

So here's to the footsteps that left us bemused,
In the theater of life, we're most often confused.
Let's tread on with joy, let the past give a cheer,
For funny missteps bring laughter, my dear!

Luminescence in the Undergrowth

Amidst the tall ferns, where oddities play,
Glow worms are giggling, lighting our way.
Their sparks are like winks, mischievous and bright,
Nature's own jokers, igniting the night.

The mushrooms are plotting some marvelous caper,
With snickers and chuckles, they dance like no taper.
They whisper old tales of the things left unsaid,
While critters engage in their fables instead.

In the shadows, still shadows, there's laughter galore,
As branches sway lightly, alluding to more.
A riddle, a puzzle, these sights to behold,
In this glowing underbrush, humor unfolds.

So let's tiptoe softly on this glimmering ground,
With laughter as our compass, let joy abound.
For in every dark corner, a flicker of light,
Shows us the funny in each silly fright.

Shadows of the Unseen

In the corners of rooms, shadows dance cheeky,
Playing hide and seek, they're delightfully sneaky.
They morph into monsters, but only for fun,
A side-splitting comedy, not to outrun.

Oh, the walls have their tales with whispers and grins,
As shadows concoct their mischievous sins.
They peek from the curtains, then dash out of sight,
With giggles and wiggles—a whimsical fright!

Partners in crime, they waltz to the tune,
Of laughter that echoes beneath the full moon.
So let's join their party; grab a friend, take a chance,
In shadows of fun, we'll all join the dance!

For life's just a play, with characters fleeting,
With shadows as friends, it's hardly completing.
Let's embrace the unseen, weave humor within,
And find joy in the corners where mischief begins.

Cadence of Longing

I searched for joy in a bowl of peas,
Only to find a cat that sneezes.
My heart it dances, it twirls in glee,
But trips on the shoelace tied to a tree.

Each time I call, my slippers respond,
They scamper away, like a magical wand.
I hold a meeting with socks that won't match,
Their secret lives, I really should catch.

A toast to the moments I can't recall,
Like that time I tried to wall climb a wall.
Laughter echoes through my baffled brain,
As I juggle my thoughts on a runaway train.

In this quirky dance of life each day,
I twirl in my socks, hip-hip-hooray!
With every stumble, there's giggles galore,
For who wouldn't laugh at a cat on the floor?

A Cascade of Fleeting Whispers

A breeze carries secrets, they giggle and shout,
My ears perk up; what's this all about?
In a game of hide and seek, I lose track,
The whispers just laugh, 'You'll never come back!'

Thoughts tumble like jellybeans in a jar,
Each color a story, each taste a bizarre.
I chase after wisdom, it slips through the air,
Like a puppy on roller skates, unaware.

In the garden of nonsense, I find my place,
Chatting with daisies – oh what a race!
They share their tales of the midnight sun,
While I giggle and slip, oh isn't this fun?

With each little chuckle, the world wobbles wide,
As I chase down the laughter that giggles inside.
The echoes of joy trip lightly, no fear,
In the fleet of the whispers, my heart finds its cheer.

Beneath the Echoing Canopy

Beneath the branches, I gather my thoughts,
The squirrels critique my creative knots.
They chatter away, judgmental and spry,
While I craft a crown of leaves for the sky.

A raccoon pops in, wearing my hat,
He strikes a pose, then scurries off flat.
With giggles and grumbles, I play my role,
A jester in nature, my heart as the goal.

Beneath leafy whispers, I ponder my fate,
As ants teem with busy plans, never too late.
They march in a line, but I'm lost in my dream,
Chasing the shadows of sunlit esteem.

With each silly thought, I dance through the trees,
While laughter bursts forth, as light as the breeze.
In this silly arena, I'm the star of the show,
And beneath the canopy, my giggles just grow.

In the Sanctuary of Shadows

In the dim light where shadows play,
A lamp dances a jig, come what may.
The curtains whisper secrets of night,
While I stumble on tales that take flight.

A sock puppet waits with an eager grin,
While I search for wisdom that's hiding within.
My reflection gives me a side-eye so sly,
I burst out in laughter and ask the 'why?'

With a jump and a twirl, I'm lost in my thoughts,
As humor weaves through the memory knots.
The shadows around me are my silly friends,
They giggle and bow, as my laughter ascends.

In this cozy theatre of mischievous dreams,
Every giggle and chuckle bursts at the seams.
In this sanctuary where the humor abounds,
Life's simple joys echo out loud in the rounds.

Cracks in the Surface

In my garden, weeds have a say,
They laugh and dance in the sun's ray.
Between the cracks, flowers tease,
Mocking my efforts with such ease.

I tried to plant a little tree,
But the squirrels thought it was for tea.
Now it grows in a crooked way,
A comedy sketch in the sunlight's play.

My neighbor thinks she's a pro,
But her daisies just put on a show.
They stand there, grinning so wide,
While I ponder what to hide.

Yet in this chaos, I find delight,
Nature's jokes, such a funny sight.
Laughter blooms where dirt has leapt,
Life's a giggle, and I've misstepped.

The Language of the Unspoken

I speak to my cat, she gives me a glare,
It's clear her thoughts are beyond compare.
She yawns at my jokes, such a droll act,
Her silence speaks volumes, that's a fact.

My plants have opinions, it seems quite bizarre,
Especially the one that grew to a star.
It turns its leaves with every new tale,
While I sit here with my coffee, pale.

I chat with my shoes, they wink in response,
Adventures await, in a goofy dance.
But the puddles laugh as I splash and flop,
In this silent exchange, laughter won't stop.

So here's to the voices we often dismiss,
Buddy cats and plants, all part of the bliss.
In a world so loud, they choose to be shy,
Yet the humor's so rich, it makes me comply.

Beneath the Surface of Thought

Beneath my worries, a joke lies in wait,
It tickles my mind, it can't help but bait.
Thought bubbles pop like a child's delight,
Whispers of wisdom take flight in the night.

I ponder the clouds, they puff up with pride,
While plotting to rain on my fun little ride.
But there's humor in thunder, a laugh in the gloom,
As lightning strikes down like a wild groom.

In the depths of my dreams, the monsters wear hats,
They invite me to tea with their grumpy old cats.
We giggle and guffaw 'til the sun starts to rise,
And the punchlines emerge as the sleep in me lies.

So here's to the frolic beneath layers so deep,
Where nonsense and laughter make memories to keep.
In the sea of my thoughts, a flotilla of cheer,
Through the waves of my mind, it all becomes clear.

The Interwoven Self

I'm many selves, a patchwork of fun,
Some are serious, while others just run.
The clown in my head pokes the thinker with glee,
Creating a circus, oh look, it's me!

In mirrors, I see reflections collide,
Each with a grin, taking nonsense in stride.
The scholar frowns at the jester's loud laugh,
But soon joins the dance, can't resist the craft.

The artist splatters colors in glee,
While the poet whispers words, wild and free.
They trade silly stories until they forget,
Who started the joke, or why they're upset.

So here's to the selves that embrace all the quirks,
Their laughter transforms like magical works.
In the tapestry crafted of giggles and cheer,
The interwoven selves bring the humor near.

Clarity Found in Shadows

In the corner, dust bunnies play,
Whispering secrets of yesterday's sway.
I trip over thoughts, oh what a shock,
Dancing like shadows on a worn-out clock.

Socks mismatched, a curious sight,
Chasing the cat through the dim twilight.
Mirrors reflect my hair in a tangle,
But I laugh it off, no need to wrangle.

A chair creaks softly, a gentle jest,
Is it the wood, or my body's quest?
With every creak, a chuckle escapes,
As my dreams teeter, in odd shapes.

Beneath the shine, there's a spark of glee,
Each corner holds a joke meant for me.
In these shadows, I find my way,
Laughter guiding me, come what may.

Beneath the Whispering Boughs

Under the tree, squirrels complain,
As they argue on who gets the grain.
Woodpeckers drum with a rhythmic beat,
While ants march in a silly retreat.

The breeze carries giggles from afar,
A game of hide-and-seek with a star.
Leaves rustle softly, they share a grin,
Disguised as wisdom but bursting with sin.

A wanderer trips over roots like a clown,
Saying, 'I swear this tree just pulled me down!'
The laughter floats high, up into the sky,
While birds play pranks, oh my, oh my!

In the shade, secrets float all around,
Each chuckle and snicker makes joy profound.
So we dance in the grass, carefree and spry,
Beneath the boughs where we're free to fly.

In the Shadows of Memory

Snapshots of times, a whimsical blur,
Old photos laughing, what's this, for sure?
Grandpa's mustache, a tree on his lip,
While Uncle Joe's shirt takes a wild trip.

Mom's trying to sing, oh what a sound!
The dog joins in, we're all spellbound.
In these moments, time takes a stroll,
Each chuckle a memory, good for the soul.

We bake some cookies, flour in my hair,
Laughter erupts, it's a sweet affair.
Burnt on the edges but love's in the mix,
These tasty disasters, oh, what a fix!

So here I sit, in laughter's embrace,
Every memory holds a funny face.
In shadows we gather, the quirky and bright,
Finding joy in the past, under moonlight.

Whispering Echoes of the Past

Echoes of laughter drift through the hall,
As Grandma yells, 'Don't you dare fall!'
I'm tangled in tales of a misfit parade,
Where socks turned into hats, quite the charade.

Pictures hang crooked, what fun to behold,
A treasure of memories, worth more than gold.
The door creaks open, a ghost with a grin,
Is that Uncle Fred or the cat with a spin?

Old games revive like a silly refrain,
Where winning is losing, and laughing's the gain.
So we gather around, a council of clowns,
With jokes and jests that bring silly frowns.

In the echoes, we find a playful embrace,
Laughter resounding, its joyful trace.
Through moments we wander, both high and low,
In whispers of past, our spirits glow.

Emerging from the Whispering Depths

I peeked into the well one day,
Thought I'd find some magic play.
But out popped a frog in a hat,
He croaked, 'Nope! I'm just a brat!'

My thoughts swam deep like fish in blue,
Each wave brought laughs, some old, some new.
But wisdom dripped like melting ice,
It hiccupped twice and said, 'Be nice!'

Bubbles floated, dancing round,
Tickling fancies where thoughts abound.
I tried to grab one, it slipped right by,
'Hey! I just wanted to say hi!'

A turtle passed with a slouchy grin,
Said, 'Life's a race, but who's to win?'
We all just chuckled and took a risk,
'Let's sip tea slow, and bask in bliss!'

The Dance of Time's Threads

Time waltzed through my little room,
In a tutu, with a broom!
I laughed so hard, I spilled my tea,
And suddenly, it danced with me!

A clock chimed in with old-time glee,
'Let's dance till the cat spills a spree!'
But before I knew it, it tripped on a shoe,
'Time waits for no one,' it squealed, 'that's true!'

We spun and twirled, oh what a sight!
Even the fridge joined with all its might.
'Thay's a party in this pantry, you see,
Just grab a snack and dance with glee!'

As the hands flew 'round in a dizzy array,
We erupted in giggles, come what may.
Time winked, 'Keep dancing through thick and thin,'
So we threw all our worries in the bin!

Unraveling the Veil of Time

I found a blanket, soft and warm,
Thought it held secrets in its charm.
Pulled a thread, and out came a sock,
I laughed so hard, nearly lost my clock!

Every tug revealed a tale,
Of fish that jumped, and ships that sail.
Then a quirky cat popped out, quite spry,
Said, 'What's time, when you can fly?'

A button rolled across the floor,
It whispered tales of distant lore.
With each stitch, a memory brews,
Of glorious snacks and silly shoes!

So here I sit, in this cuddly spree,
Unraveling laughs, just like candy.
The blanket giggles with every tease,
As I drink my tea, feeling quite at ease!

Underneath the Whispering Winds

Beneath the trees, I bent to hear,
The whispers of leaves, oh so near.
They giggled and chuckled like small kids,
'What's your secret? Do tell, you whiz!'

A breeze tickled my ear like a tease,
'Life's a grand joke, if you please!'
With every rustle, a punchline formed,
Even the squirrels danced, well-informed!

A snail scoffed, 'I'm in no rush!'
Yet in the distance, a twig went 'thush!'
We compared notes on slow and fast,
And laughed at the future, waltzing past.

So here we lounge, in nature's embrace,
With whispers of joy, we find our place.
Under the canopy, life's game we play,
With laughter and tales brightening the day!

www.ingramcontent.com/pod-product-compliance
Lightning Source LLC
Chambersburg PA
CBHW071850160426
43209CB00003B/497